QUIET ACHIEVERS

THE NEW ZEALAND PATH
TO REFORM

QUIET ACHIEVERS

THE NEW ZEALAND PATH TO REFORM

Oliver Hartwich

Connor Court Publishing

PO Box 224W
Ballarat VIC 3350
sales@connorcourt.com
www.connorcourt.com

ISBN: 9781925138429 (pbk.)

Cover design by Ian James

Printed in Australia

'The prime art of politics is that of a persuasion which
cuts deep into the popular mind and heart.'

Sir Robert Gordon Menzies

The R. G. Menzies Essays

The R. G. Menzies Essays is an occasional series of monographs commissioned by the Menzies Research Centre as a reasoned contribution to the formation of enlightened policy.

Correspondence is welcome and will be considered for publication in future volumes.

Series Editor: Nick Cater

Series Publisher: Connor Court

The Menzies Research Centre

The Menzies Research Centre is dedicated to the improvement of public policy through the application of the enduring liberal principles of freedom, enterprise reason and opportunity.

The MRC is non-profit organisation funded by public grants and private philanthropy. It is philosophically aligned to the foundation principles of the Liberal Party of Australia.

Web address: www.menziesrc.org

Correspondence: correspondence@menziesrc.org

PO Box 6091

Kingston ACT 2604

Australia

Phone: +61 2 6273 5608

CONTENTS

About the author

Dr Oliver Hartwich is the Executive
Director of The New Zealand Initiative
(*www.nzinitiative.org.nz*), an independent
public policy think tank supported by
chief executives of major New Zealand
businesses.

Before joining the Initiative, he was
a Research Fellow at the Centre for Independent Studies (Sydney),
the Chief Economist at Policy Exchange (London), and an advisor
in the UK House of Lords. His publications have covered a wide
range of topics, including housing, transport, local government, and
global economic issues. He holds a Master's degree in Economics
and Business Administration and a Ph.D. in Law from Bochum
University (Germany).

Dr Hartwich is a frequent media commentator and writes
popular columns in the *Business Spectator* (Melbourne) and the
National Business Review (Auckland). His articles have been published
by major newspapers in Britain, Germany, Switzerland, Australia
and New Zealand.

Acknowledgements / Disclaimer

The author wishes to thank Nick Cater and the Menzies Research Centre for the invitation to write this essay. Thanks are due to the team of The New Zealand Initiative for providing valuable feedback and comments – in particular Jenesa Jeram, Dr Eric Crampton, Dr Bryce Wilkinson, Chelsy Blair and Roger Partridge. Last but not least, many thanks to Julie Hartwich for her support.

Views in this paper are those of the author and do not necessarily reflect the views of The New Zealand Initiative, its staff, advisors, members, directors of officers. All remaining errors are the sole responsibility of the author.

Foreword 1

Nick Cater

Sir Robert Menzies once said that the hardest part of politics was persuading people to take a long-range view. If so, it is tempting to conclude that politics is a dying art in much of the Western democratic world.

In the aftermath of the 2008 global credit crisis, the need for drastic structural reform in developed economies became inescapable. The challenge of an ageing population, accumulating debt, unsustainable government spending, stagnant productivity and bureaucratic inefficiency are not peculiar to Australia. Yet here, as in almost every developed economy, structural reform has proved elusive in recent years.

Yet there are signs that New Zealand may be bucking the trend by making a concerted effort to reduce the size of government, enhance the scope for growth and tackle seemingly intractable problems in tax, welfare and government spending. That the reforms of John Key's government have been barely noticed on this side of the Tasman is a clue to their success. Incremental change has been a deliberate tactic; Key and his team have concentrated on getting the job done and letting the benefits of reform speak for themselves.

In doing so, Key has broken the mould of previous centre-Right reforming governments in the Western democracies that made a virtue of toughness and portrayed short term-pain as the necessary price for long-term gain. Instead, Key has attempted to reform from the centre, preferring consensus to confrontation.

Oliver Hartwich's perceptive essay offers an authoritative account of a period of reform in New Zealand that contrasts sharply with the political climate in Australia over the last six years. As a policy analyst who has worked in both Europe and Australia, Hartwich is in a good position to judge whether the technique he describes as 'incremental radicalism' could be applied elsewhere.

He concludes that Tony Abbott's government would do well to study the New Zealand experience. There is much to admire in both the substance and execution of reforms. The most important lesson, however, may be simply this: reform fatigue is not a permanent condition. Despite all the pressures of modern politics, it is still possible for a skillful and determined government to leave a country in better shape than the one it inherited.

November 2014

Foreword 2

Ruth Richardson

'Brand Key' swept to victory in 2014 with a majority unprecedented since the introduction of New Zealand's mixed-member proportional electoral system.

In *Quiet Achievers*, John Key's political playbook is dissected in a comprehensive but acute fashion. The monograph serves as something of a primer to the Australian body politic as the country is forced to break its long reform holiday.

Oliver Hartwich recognises the constraints of a proportional representation regime from his background in Germany. He attributes John Key's success, achieved against the electoral odds, to the practice of 'incremental radicalism'.

As an unashamed practitioner of big-bang radical reform, this monograph prompts two observations, one complimentary and one cautionary. I offer plaudits to Key for rehabilitating the vocation of politics. It is an encouraging precedent; if only more skilled business types were willing to enter the political arena.

The cautionary tale is that the pace and scope of reform is a function of the prevailing imperatives. When bold-course correction is called for incrementalism just doesn't cut it. NZ and Australia would be much diminished had not those bold strokes occurred in the previous reform eras.

As both countries grapple with the challenges of the new millennium, *Quiet Achievers* is a reminder that, as the wags once put it, reform is not a one-night stand.

Ruth Richardson was Finance Minister of New Zealand from 1990 to 1993.

Introduction

When Tony Abbott became Australia's 28th Prime Minister in September 2013, an editorial in *The Australian* newspaper outlined his challenge:

> Economic and fiscal policy should have first call on Mr Abbott's attention. Australia's reform holiday has lasted well over a decade now, spanning the last years of John Howard's government and the entire period of Labor. For the sake of our future prosperity, Mr Abbott cannot become the fourth prime minister in succession to adopt a lackadaisical attitude to economic reform. Without substantial productivity gains, Australia will be a net loser from the much proclaimed Asian century.[1]

The view that Australia has lost the will to implement meaningful reforms is widespread. The phrase 'reform holiday', which *The Australian* used in its editorial, is a good description of what Australia has experienced since the beginning of the century. The 1980s and 1990s were years of economic modernisation that marked, to quote Paul Kelly's phrase, 'the end of certainty'.[2] What followed was a period in which the achievements of the past were maintained but not extended.

The last substantial reform deserving of that name was the introduction of the Goods and Services Tax in July 2000. Tellingly, it had its origins in a proposal presented to the 1985 Tax Summit by a Labor treasurer, Paul Keating. It was left to John Howard, however, to complete this particular bit of unfinished business in his second term in the face of Labor opposition. The compromises required to achieve majority support in the Senate prevented the GST from becoming more broad-based, as Howard explains in his autobiography.[3]

Since then, Australian interest in further reforming the economy and becoming more competitive has declined. Why it has declined is a matter for debate. Suffice to say it must rediscover the art of reform or face the consequences: a reduction in relative prosperity and a decline in opportunities.

One possible cause of reform fatigue is the mining boom which drove the wider economy by generating income, jobs and tax revenue. It coincided with a housing boom that helped create a false sense of economic security and an illusion of prosperity. Add to that the economic spill-overs from the rise of Asia in general and China in particular, and it is easy to see how Australians lost their appetite for tough and painful reforms. The economy seemed to be doing well without them.

Though this argument certainly holds for the first years of the century, the Global Financial Crisis came as a reminder that Australia cannot afford to rest on its laurels. Faced with this exogenous shock, the Australian economy was treated to substantial fiscal and monetary stimulus measures. The resulting growth, however, was as small as the government deficits were large.[4]

The years since the onset of the GFC have also seen a decline in the favourable terms-of-trade Australia enjoyed in the mining boom years. This means that Australia could no longer take future growth for granted. It cannot just speculate on windfall gains arising from ever-increasing demand for its commodity exports.

In these circumstances, it should have been easier to argue the case for economic reform and continue where John Howard had left off in 2000. Yet Australia refused to interrupt its reform holiday and continued almost as if nothing had changed. Instead of tackling the issues crying out to be addressed – industrial relations, fiscal policy, the tax system and federalism immediately come to mind – Australia experienced bitter political battles that were fought rather over personalities than over policies.

Against this background, it is hardly surprising that some observers despair of the political system and its ability to deliver good government. After leaving politics, former finance minister Lindsay Tanner published a good account of the distractions provided by the media, which often prevent serious political discussions.[5] In his latest book *Triumph and Demise*, Paul Kelly also argues that serious economic reform is practically impossible in the modern era. He cites the pressures of 24 hour news and a headline and focus groups obsessed culture that have contributed to the increased polarisation of politics and the deterioration of tried and trusted political method.[6] Kelly has long argued that the great age of reform described in *The End of Certainty* appears to be over and that we are left with a political system unable to produce solid, wealth enhancing policy.

The profound sense of pessimism about Australia's ability to reform is palpable. It seems as if the kind of big and bold policy changes that were possible a generation ago are no longer feasible. And it is not just in Australia, it must be said, where the age of reform is over. The contrasts between Ronald Reagan and Barack Obama or Margaret Thatcher and David Cameron could not be more striking; on the one hand, the conviction politicians of the 1980s who almost single-handedly turned around their countries;

on the other the less ideologically committed, more pragmatic ditherers of today. Where reforms do happen in Western democracies, for example in parts of the Eurozone, they only do so out of dire necessity. However, they are usually not driven by politicians' commitment to a reformist intellectual framework.

Politicians, to be fair, are not the only ones to blame. Selling policy change, even when it is clearly needed, has become harder as special interest groups have become more vocal and organised. There is too much institutional inertia in Western democracies – and too great a risk to lose office when going too far beyond what voters are willing to accept. In the famous words of former Luxembourg Prime Minister and new EU Commission President Jean-Claude Juncker: 'We all know what to do, we just don't know how to get re-elected after we've done it.'[7]

The question, therefore, has to be whether economic reform at the beginning of the 21st century is still possible. Or, asked differently, whether Western democracy has become too streamlined, polished and poll-driven to preclude the implementation of the kinds of measures that are unpopular in the short-term and yet necessary to lay the foundations of long-term recovery and growth.

While Australia and other countries were pondering these questions, New Zealand went to the polls on 20 September 2014 and re-elected the government of John Key for a third term. The Key administration is the most reform-minded and economically liberal New Zealand has seen in a generation – at least in the eyes of many Australian observers. Viewed from the across the Tasman the New Zealand experience offers encouragement that economic reform is still possible. Perhaps Australia's aversion to reform may be a temporary and local phenomena.

Writing in *The Australian*, economist Henry Ergas credited Key's exceptional political management skills that allowed him to implement an ambitious agenda for change:

> The [election] result attests to the merits of Key's policies: a prudent fiscal strategy, which will see New Zealand return to surplus sooner than Australia, despite being harder hit by the global financial crisis and having to bear the immense costs of reconstructing Christchurch; far-reaching tax reform, which reduced income taxes and raised the GST; and a continued emphasis on controlling public spending, including by better targeting social welfare. Together with cautious changes to industrial relations, injecting greater flexibility into the Employment Relations Act Key inherited from Labour, those policies have helped lift the country's growth rate to a stellar near 4 percent.[8]

The *Sydney Morning Herald's* international editor Peter Hartcher portrayed Key not only as an astute political player but also as a politician driven by radical beliefs:

> Key has been a neo-liberal activist who has administered some distasteful pills. He raised the rate of the NZ GST from 12.5 percent to 15 percent. He has been part-privatising state assets. He's tightened eligibility for welfare payments. At the same time, he's cut the top income tax rate from 38 percent to 33. You might not like his politics or his ideology. But he has coaxed his country into swallowing the pills of reform yet entrusting him with power once again.[9]

Reading through accounts of New Zealand's recent developments like Hartcher's, one might get the impression that Key is a kind of 21st century Ronald Reagan or Margaret Thatcher, working through an economically liberal agenda to substantially change his country. Indeed, if one enumerates the reforms undertaken by Key's government, it sounds impressive.

Interestingly, however, hardly any New Zealand commentator (with the exception of some on the extreme Left) would subscribe to such an interpretation. Indeed the Prime Minister would never self-identify as a Thatcherite, neo-liberal reformer.

The *National Business Review's* Rob Hosking summed up the platform on which John Key's National Party stood in the 2014 election:

> [A] broad, not particularly specific continuation of what National has done since taking power at the end of 2008: a constrained public sector and gradualist reform of areas such as education, employment, and the environment. The model has been that of John Howard's 1996-2007 Liberal governments in Australia: gradual reform but taking the population with those reforms rather than imposing radical reform and alienating a generation, as has happened in New Zealand in the past.[10]

The reference to John Howard is apt, not least because Key and Howard are personally close. Key, like Howard, is cautious to avoid setting an over-ambitious agenda, suggesting he is more of a conservative than a diehard economic liberal. After winning the 2014 election, Key was keen to emphasise his steady approach saying, 'I don't intend to take the party veering off to the right. We've held the centre ground for the last six years. We're not looking to do radical things.' Instead, he promised to preside over an administration 'that governs for all New Zealanders'.[11] It was a clear rejection of demands from the business community in particular to use his mandate to increase the speed of reform.

Looking at New Zealand and the government of John Key, especially from an Australian perspective, presents something of a paradox. How can a government that appears to be ultra-reformist and (neo-) liberal to Australian observers be regarded as moderate in New Zealand? How come Australians see Key as a radical change agent in the mould of Jeff Kennett while New Zealanders prefer to compare him to the more gradualist John Howard? Could Australians be projecting a yearning for political leadership at home on New Zealand's popular Prime Minister?

This essay will examine the economic record of New Zealand under John Key's government, and it will draw comparisons and parallels with Australia. In doing so, we will be able to identify what, if anything, Australia could learn from the New Zealand experience and examine the prospects for further reforms on both sides of the Tasman.

The Key government's reform agenda

If Key intended to be a radical reformer, he hid his ambitions well. There was no sweeping agenda for change after his election in 2008. On the contrary; his new government deliberately downplayed expectations that they would radically depart from the previous administration's agenda. Almost all of the programs introduced by Helen Clark's government were left untouched. Key ensured that economic management did not become the main campaign issue in the 2008 election, running instead on a platform promising a continuation of the Labour agenda, but with younger and fresher faces.

Key's National Party was prepared to live with Labour's legacy, including the Cullen Fund (New Zealand's sovereign wealth fund), interest-free student loans, a legal entitlement to four weeks' paid annual leave and Working for Families tax credits. There were no plans to privatise the state owned enterprises Kiwibank and KiwiRail. Nothing, it appeared, would be allowed to scare off voters who, after nine years of Labour, had only just returned the National Party to power. The signal was that Key intended to lead a moderate government – and a government that no-one had to be afraid of.

Downplaying any kind of change may have been good politics.

As Luke Malpass, then a researcher at the Centre for Independent Studies in Sydney, wrote at the time:

> Politicians are not often popular for making big economic reforms and Key has largely refrained from doing so. Indeed, unlike Australia, 'reform' is basically a political swearword in New Zealand. ... Indeed, along with his policy timidity, Key's political style is the opposite of the Gillard government. Instead of regularly making inane announcements, his government quietly gets on with implementing its modest promises and plans. Instead of repeating infantile slogans, Key answers questions, and admits error or ignorance.[12]

It was easy to get the impression in Key's first term was that he was a Prime Minister nervous about change. When challenged on his modest-sounding agenda, Key repeatedly said that he did not have a mandate for anything he had not taken to the election. Besides, the times were unsettling enough. These were the years of the Global Financial Crisis, with the collapse of big financial institutions and entire countries defaulting on their loans. In this climate, any government could be forgiven for demonstrating a commitment to stability instead of adding to the public's feeling of uncertainty.

Yet beneath Key's public modesty and humility was an ambition to create an environment conducive to change when circumstances allowed. The groundwork for major policy shifts was laid during Key's first term, and no other area better demonstrates this careful preparation than welfare.

Expected to work

In April 2010, the government established the Welfare Working Group, a body of experts tasked with reviewing the operations of the welfare state. The goal was 'to examine ways to reduce long-term benefit dependency in New Zealand for people of working age'.[13] The review had a wide remit allowing it to investigate welfare arrangements for 'sole parents, sick people, disabled people and other people at risk of long-term benefit dependency.' In other words, this was to be a root-and-branch assessment of the welfare state that would not be contented with limited and superficial quick fixes.

When the Welfare Working Group delivered its final report on 22 February 2011, the government got what it wanted. The announcement of its 43 recommendations for policy change was overshadowed by the Canterbury earthquake which struck on the same day. As far as welfare policy was concerned, however, the recommendations were an earthquake in themselves. The whole edifice of the New Zealand welfare state would be shaken by it.

The group recommended that a range of different benefit categories be replaced by a new Jobseeker Support benefit. The ambition was already reflected in the name. This was a benefit whose very purpose it was to make itself redundant. Instead of keeping benefit recipients on welfare, they were now expected to move into paid labour as quickly as possible. Long-term welfare would be drastically reduced, and to encourage this process beneficiaries would face reciprocal obligations, making it harder to remain on welfare.

The recommendations were far-reaching and ambitious. So ambitious, in fact, that they allowed Key to portray himself as a moderate by rejecting the most radical proposal: an obligation on single parents to return to work when their youngest child turns 14 weeks. Nevertheless, Key was able to recalibrate the welfare state by accepting most of the remaining recommendations.

In the lead-up to the 2011 election, Key therefore made it clear that he accepted the Group's analysis that welfare had become too generous and widespread and promised broad changes for his second term: 'It's important we signal to New Zealanders that if we are afforded a second term that there will be reform in welfare,'[14] he said in May 2011.

After the 2011 election, Key and his Minister of Social Development and Employment, Paula Bennett, set out to implement the welfare reforms. Bennett's authority to speak on these issues was enhanced by her personal background. At age 17, she had become a single mother, raising her daughter on welfare. She worked her way up by working in tourism, waitressing at a truck stop, cleaning, a receptionist at a hair salon and finally at a rest home as a dishwasher and a nurse aide before studying social work. No-one could have claimed that the government's welfare reforms were designed by armchair theorists. The minister in charge knew exactly what she was talking about, and not even her critics would doubt Paula Bennett's passion or sincerity.[15]

The welfare reforms were introduced in stages. In a first stage, announced in February 2012, the focus was on changing expectations. Sole parents with children five years and older would be required to be available for part-time work, while sole parents with children 14 and older had to make themselves available for full-time employment. Similar expectations were placed on women receiving the Widow's and Women Alone benefits and on partners of beneficiaries with children. Sole parents who had another child while on a benefit now were required to make themselves available for work after one year, thus discouraging the option of welfare as a career.

The second stage of the government's welfare reforms was the streamlining of benefit types, as suggested by the Welfare Working Group. Three new benefit types replaced seven previous benefit categories. For the majority of beneficiaries, the expectation was to be available to move back into the labour market. Only people who are severely restricted or unable to work on a long-term basis because of a health condition or disability, or those caring for someone who needs significant care, were granted exemption. All other welfare recipients were placed on either the new Jobseeker Support or Sole Parent Support benefit with varying expectations to work.[16]

Additional social obligations were placed on beneficiaries. Children from benefit-dependent homes now had to be enrolled in early childhood education from age three, primary school at age five and also had to be enrolled with a doctor. Job-seekers were required to be drug-free, with funding made available to employers and training providers to test beneficiaries for drugs.

The narrative the government built around its welfare reforms was one of assistance rather than punishment. They would be doing beneficiaries a kindness by helping them return to the labour market. Bennett announced:

> We should be supporting beneficiaries to move off benefits where possible, so they can have a better quality of life and more choices... Instead of just handing benefits over and leaving people to their own devices, the National-led Government is taking an active approach because we have

greater aspirations for New Zealanders and their children, achieved through work, not welfare.'[17]

An emphasis on investment was another key part of the government's reform agenda. Under the so-called 'investment approach' the average lifetime costs of every welfare recipients were calculated and social services were directed to focus their efforts on those with the highest likely lifetime costs.[18]

When actuaries calculated the lifetime cost of all people on benefits their findings were revealing. The total lifetime cost of all benefit recipients was calculated to be NZ$78 billion, but recipients of unemployment benefits made up only five percent of that amount. The most expensive beneficiaries were those on sole parents (23%), sickness (9%) and invalid's benefits (24%).

The actuarial valuation also concluded that a total of just 4,000 16- and 17-year-olds on benefits accounted for $1 billion of the lifetime welfare costs. According to further government calculations, teen parents spend an average of 19 years on benefits at a cost of around NZ$246,000 over a lifetime to taxpayers.[19] The government therefore argued that investments should be made to help those people off benefits first that would cause the greatest cost to the public purse if they were left to a "welfare career".

Benefit	September 2009	September 2013	September 2014
Jobseeker Support	143,628	126,470	123,133
Sole Parent Support	85,319	79,699	72,589
Supported Living Payment	91,342	92,072	93,852
Youth Payment/ Young Parent Payment	1,486	1,293	1,335
Other	5,036	4,860	3,412
Total working-age recipients	326,811	304,394	294,321
Percentage of working-age population	12.30%	11.20%	10.70%

Figure 1: Summary of working-age clients receiving main benefits,
end of September 2009, 2013 and 2014[20]

The Ministry for Social Development summed up the investment approach policy and its success so far in their Annual Report:

> We are using an annual actuarial valuation to manage the lifetime liability of the benefit system more effectively. This gives us greater ability to identify clients in terms of their projected lifetime patterns of benefit receipt. The latest valuation of the welfare system, at 30 June 2013, puts the lifetime liability of the benefit system at $76.5 billion – a decrease of $10.3 billion from $86.8 billion in 2012. Of the decrease, $4.4 billion can be attributed to our interventions.

In 2013/2014, our investment strategy focused on clients
with work obligations who had a medium to high risk of
ongoing long-term welfare dependency. We developed
targeted trials to help determine which services and support
work best to achieve appropriate quality of life or work-
readiness goals for this group.[21]

The reduction in the calculated life-time costs of welfare also
shows in the absolute number of welfare recipients, as Figure 1
shows. While the reduction in the number of jobseekers from 2013
to 2014 may also be due to the overall development of the economy,
the 9 percent reduction in people on sole parent support in a single
year is likely a result of the welfare reform's policy changes.

While the overall reduction in Jobseeker Support recipients
may not look too large at first sight, it is interesting to note that
progress has been made on long-term recipients of this particular
benefit. The government had set itself a target of reducing the
number of people who had been on Jobseeker Support for more
than 12 months by 30 percent, from 78,000 in April 2012 to 55,000
by June 2017. As Figure 2 suggests, this could well be achieved by
then, if not earlier.

The manner in which welfare reform was implemented
demonstrated remarkable political skill. Instead of rushing a radical
reform agenda through parliament, the government allowed the
Welfare Working Group to lay the ground. The minister responsible
for implementation could credibly defend the changes based
on her own personal experience. The government established a
narrative that emphasised the positive effects to beneficiaries, who
would be given better life options, as well as for the taxpayers. Both
perspectives are held together by the much promoted "investment
approach", which provided the intellectual framework for all
government agencies.

No.

90,000

85,000

80,000

75,000

70,000   **75,366**
              March 2013

65,000   **68,932**
                              March 2014
60,000

55,000

50,000   **Target**
                                                        June 2017
45,000

40,000
      Jun-10   Jun-11   Jun-12   Jun-13   Jun-14   Jun-15   Jun-16   Jun-17

Figure 2: Number of people continuously on Jobseeker Support benefits for over 12 months[22]

By presenting far-reaching welfare reforms in this carefully constructed context, those who resisted the changes were made to seem radical, rather than the government. The pressure group Auckland Action Against Poverty called the reforms the 'biggest boot in the guts' to beneficiaries for decades[23], while the Labour opposition claimed that the 'reforms just tear up the idea of the social contract'.[24] Such language was not only over-the-top, but it contrasted markedly with the apparent benevolence of the government which was committed to helping people off welfare and into a better life.

Thus the Key government was able to make changes to welfare that had eluded other developed countries. In Germany far less ambitious changes had precipitated the downfall of Chancellor Gerhard Schröder, reducing his Social Democrat Party to a shadow of its former self.[25] The difference was that Key had carefully choreographed his moves and better communicated reform agenda.

Key's reform took time and preparation but once introduced were accepted by large parts of the public – an acceptance that will grow if the current trend welfare dependency reduction continues.

The patient English

After the election of the National-led government in late 2008, the toughest job in John Key's cabinet went to Bill English. He became Minister of Finance and Deputy Prime Minister at the peak of the Global Financial Crisis, just a couple of months after the collapse of Lehman Brothers. Three weeks into his job, he received a pessimistic economic update from Treasury that reflected the turbulence of international financial markets. Gross government debt, which had been only 17.5 percent of GDP in 2008, was forecast to nearly double to 33.1 percent by 2013. Real GDP per capita was forecast to shrink for the next two years (-0.6 percent in 2009 and -0.2 percent in 2010). Over the same time, unemployment was predicted to climb from 4.7 to 6.2 percent.[26] These were certainly not the easiest of times to be put in charge of economic policy.

The bad news kept coming. Standard & Poor's downgraded New Zealand's outlook to negative in January 2009,[27] and both the OECD and the IMF presented gloomy forecasts for the New Zealand economy in early 2009.[28]

It was a combination of domestic and international factors and risks, none of which were easy to predict let alone manage. The IMF summed up the multiple challenges for New Zealand by pointing to a

> significant deterioration in the global outlook in recent months, and the likely spillover effects that the global

downturn may have on New Zealand. Households are constrained by high debt levels, falling house and equity prices, and uncertain employment prospects. Business investment is held back by a fall in confidence, weaker profitability, and tighter credit conditions. Downside risks in the outlook are high and linked to the unprecedented uncertainties surrounding the depth and duration of the global recession.[29]

As if these challenges were not difficult enough, New Zealand was faced with the devastating Canterbury earthquakes. On 4 September 2010 a magnitude 7.1 earthquake occurred in the South Island near Christchurch, which was followed by a series of damaging aftershocks over the following months. The most severe aftershock was a shallow 6.3 earthquake close to the centre of Christchurch on 22 February 2011, which resulted in 185 deaths and destroyed large parts of the city.

The Canterbury earthquakes were New Zealand's largest peacetime disaster and their economic impact was severe. In 2013, the government estimated the total cost of the recovery to be around NZ$ 40 billion, with a fiscal cost of NZ$ 15 billion.[30]

When assessing the New Zealand government's fiscal management since 2008, it is important to keep reminding oneself of these challenges. The past six years were no ordinary years by any standard – not for New Zealand, and not for the global economy. Quite on the contrary, it is fair to say that it has been the most troubled time for the world economy since at least the oil crises of the 1970s or maybe even since the Great Depression of the 1930s. The impacts of the financial crisis which started in the US subprime lending market have been felt far and wide, and the ongoing European debt crisis certainly has not made things any easier.

Australians are of course only too well aware of what these crises did to their own public finances. The Rudd/Gillard governments' expansionary fiscal policy turned Australia's public finances a deep shade of red, despite the mining and terms-of-trade boom Australia enjoyed, and without the kinds of natural disasters that New Zealand experienced in the Canterbury earthquakes. (As an aside, the 2010/11 Queensland floods were a much less damaging event at an estimated cost of A$ 5.6 billion and served as a justification for the introduction of a temporary surcharge on income tax, the so-called Flood Levy.[31])

For a government looking for an excuse to ramp up spending, taxes and deficits, the circumstances that New Zealand faced over the past years offered plenty. In times of real (and sometimes also in imagined) national emergencies such as wars, natural disasters and recessions, governments often expand markedly, as economist and historian Robert Higgs explained in his classic treatise *Crisis and Leviathan*.[32] However, in New Zealand's case all these crises did not fuel Leviathan's appetite. To a large degree, this is English's most impressive achievement.

As Figure 3 shows, with the exception of an earthquake-caused spike in expenditure for 2011, the New Zealand government managed to keep both current revenue and operating expenditure relatively steady as a percentage of GDP since 2009. In fact, since 2011 the expenditure ratio has fallen the below 2009 level, and the government is on target to get the budget back to surplus in the current fiscal year (2014/15).

New Zealand government budget
(percent of GDP)

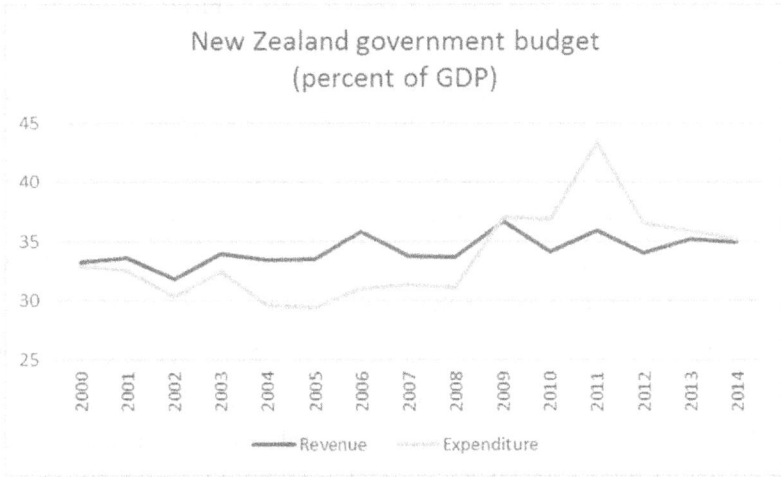

Figure 3: New Zealand government budget (Source: International Monetary Fund)

Figure 4 is based on the New Zealand Treasury's 2014 pre-election update forecasts. On the Treasury's current projected trajectory, government spending (excluding finance costs, and accrued and realised gains and losses on capital items) will fall to below 27 percent of GDP by 2028, albeit while increasing government

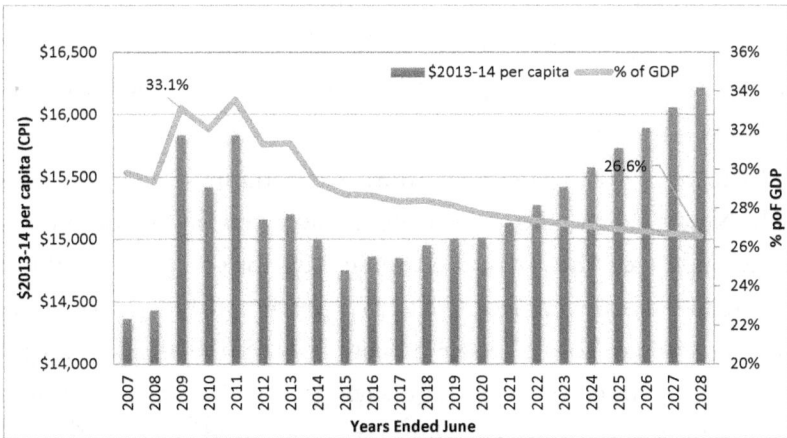

Figure 4: Forecast of core Crown operating expenditure excluding finance costs
(Source: NZ Treasury/ own calculations)[33]

spending in constant price per capita terms. Holding down the growth in nominal government spending below the growth of economic output would allow the government to shrink the size of the state over time while actually increasing government spending in absolute per capita terms. It would be hard to oppose this strategy since it requires neither budget cuts nor austerity measures. Government provision of public goods would continue to rise faster than population growth. However, it would ensure that government will eventually represent a smaller proportion of the economy.

The first two budgets of the National-led government under John Key in 2009 and 2010 included some new spending measures but from then on the government presented a series of so-called 'zero budgets'. This meant that any new programmes had to be funded from cuts elsewhere – a strategy to impose spending discipline on departments.

New Zealand's response to the GFC was more muted than Australia's. Where the Rudd government in 2009 introduced a 'shock-and-awe' stimulus package of A$42 billion,[34] New Zealand's measures comprised of a modest NZ$323.3 million home insulation and clean heating campaign and NZ$50 million for a new national cycleway network.

Instead of going down a more expenditure-driven stimulus path, New Zealand chose a different way by cutting income taxes in the middle of the crisis: the top tax rate for someone on about $NZ45,000 a year went from 33 to 17.5 percent, the top income-tax rate was slashed from 39 to 33 percent at NZ$70,000, aligned with the trust tax rate. To encourage savings ahead of consumption, GST (which applies to everything) was increased from 12.5 to 15 percent. Company tax was reduced to 28 percent.

The New Zealand government realised it had little room for fiscal manoeuvre if it was to avoid an explosion in public debt. It was obliged to find other ways of helping the economy through the crisis. Employing people was made easier, for example through the introduction of a 90 day probationary working period in employment law. Compulsory employer co-contributions to KiwiSaver, New Zealand's voluntary retirement savings scheme, were temporarily reduced from 4 percent to 2 percent and increased later to 3 percent as conditions improved.

On presenting the 2009 budget, when the whole rest of the developed world was in crisis, stimulus and bail-out mode, Bill English declared that his budget was "a balanced response to the recession" and stressed that it took "the first steps towards improving productivity and competitiveness in the longer term."[35] The signal from statements like this was meant to be that this was a government that did not panic in the sight of crisis but remained focused on policies that would improve New Zealand's economic performance over time. Perhaps this strategic, patient approach did more to restore business confidence in New Zealand than all the frantic policy activity on the other side of the Tasman.

Bill English also benefitted from the establishment of a new institution, which resulted from the 2008 Confidence and Supply Agreement between John Key's National Party and ACT, a small classical liberal party.[36] ACT had pushed for a New Zealand Productivity Commission, analogous to the Australian Productivity Commission, which was subsequently established by an Act of Parliament in 2010 and formally commenced work in April 2011.

The Productivity Commission is an independent Crown entity, however it receives the vast majority of its funding (around 90 percent) for work on inquiries determined by the government. The topics of its first inquiries suggest that the government is using the Commission strategically in order to prepare the ground for subsequent reforms:

- Using land for housing
- More effective social services
- Regulatory institutions and practices
- Boosting services sector productivity
- Local government regulation
- Trans-Tasman joint study
- Housing affordability
- International freight transport services

In this way, the Productivity Commission is playing the role of the government's own think tank. It is noteworthy that despite its young age, it is currently already undertaking its third inquiry into housing and local government-related affairs. This is certainly not coincidental; Bill English has long been an outspoken advocate of housing, planning and local government reforms. As he wrote in a foreword to Demographia's annual housing affordability survey in 2013:

> Housing affordability is complex in the detail – governments intervene in many ways – but is conceptually simple. It costs too much and takes too long to build a house in New Zealand. Land has been made artificially scarce by regulation that locks up land for development. This regulation has made land supply unresponsive to demand. ... From the Government's perspective, worsening housing affordability creates a number of problems. Fiscal pressures increase because financial assistance for housing is tied to its market price. Home ownership provides financial security and a form of savings and lowers dependence on public assistance

later in life. Worsening affordability increases demands for direct intervention through rent controls and public housing. We are aware of the results of these sorts of interventions overseas and must avoid them.[37]

It is quite likely that housing and planning policies will be the next area of economic reform in New Zealand. Over the past years, Bill English has not left any doubts that he is convinced of the need to act on housing supply. The intellectual case for reform has been made in a series of reports not only by the Productivity Commission but also by The New Zealand Initiative think tank. With the ground now prepared, a broad consensus has been established that New Zealand has a supply-side problem which needs to be addressed.

Bill English has interpreted his role as Minister of Finance wide, going well beyond his core responsibility of balancing the government's books. He presents himself as the government's economic strategist, taking a long-term view of New Zealand's competitive position. It was this long-term approach which spared New Zealand the fiscal excesses which could have resulted from the GFC and the Canterbury earthquakes. The same kind of strategic thinking affects New Zealand's business confidence and economic competitiveness. Without doubt, the patient Mr English, who assumed his role under the most difficult circumstances, has become the greatest adornment to Key's cabinet.

The International Monetary Fund's gloomy assessment just five years ago has been superseded by much more optimistic story:

> The economic expansion is becoming increasingly embedded and broad-based, with growth exceeding 3 percent in the second half of 2013. The drivers include supportive financial conditions, record high export commodity prices,

resurgent construction activity related to the Canterbury post-earthquake rebuild and general housing shortages, and a substantial increase in net immigration. Business and consumer confidence indicators have risen to the highest levels since the global financial crisis. The labor market continues to strengthen with the unemployment rate falling to 6 percent despite increasing labor force participation.[38]

For an economy that not so long ago seemed destined to years of deficits and stagnations, this is a remarkable turnaround.

Incremental radicalism

Key therefore should be seen as a reformist Prime Minister who is moving his country in the direction of economic liberalism. Yet in none of the areas in which New Zealand has been reforming over the past six years could the Prime Minister be described as the spearhead of reform. Key usually remains in the background, leaving it to his ministers to make the case for policy changes, and then, as public support is building up, takes a more active role in selling the policy to the electorate.

Key's reluctance to initiate or lead reform debates could be interpreted as lack of conviction, and indeed this is what some of his critics claim. Rodney Hide, for example, was a minister in Key's first cabinet for the ACT party and is now a columnist with the *National Business Review*. In one of his recent columns, Hide delivered a broadside at Key:

> We like to grumble about the way things are. But we don't like change. Mr Key captures the public mood perfectly. He's giving us exactly what we want: nothing but the status quo. Politicians with ideas scare us. There's no chance Mr Key will scare us. He has his power precisely because he does nothing with it.[39]

Like an impressionist painting, the reforming pattern of the Key government is more easily seen from a distance. It may explain why the current New Zealand government appears from Australia as a good, reformist role model to follow. In New Zealand meanwhile, this aspect of Key's government is deliberately (and successfully) played down by Key himself. Key lets others prepare the reforms; he lets others implement them; and he will certainly talk about positive results of his policies but he will never engage in any kind of reform rhetoric which to parts of the electorate would be alienating.

Key is playing this popularity game extraordinarily successfully; indeed, by some accounts, he is the most popular leader in the developed world. Should he manage to stay in power for a fourth or maybe a fifth term, he would have a chance of leaving an impressive legacy.

Yet tension is inherent in the Key model. The constant demand for electoral popularity precludes him from tackling necessary but unpopular reforms. New Zealand's overly complex rules on foreign direct investment, for example, are a millstone around the economy's neck. Yet the issue attracts strong emotions, especially when farmland is concerned, and Key is unlikely to touch it. Adjusting the superannuation age in line with increasing longevity or scrapping interest-free loans to students are other necessary changes that are unlikely to be made for as long as Key remains Prime Minister.

Key's incremental radicalism, then, is an attempt to balance the conflicting ambitions of securing political power and effecting economic change. For now at least it seems to be working to the benefit of Key personally, his party politically, and New Zealand economically.

Closing the Trans-Tasman gap?

Only until a couple of years ago, it would have been unthinkable to suggest that New Zealand could hold some policy lessons for Australia, let alone that it could be seen as a model that Australia might wish to emulate. Australians have become used to regarding New Zealanders as their poorer cousins. Rather than wonder what was right in New Zealand, they were conditioned to ask what was wrong.[43]

New Zealanders shared the idea that the grass was indeed greener – metaphorically at least – on the Western side of the Tasman. They voted with their feet; in some years the equivalent of almost one

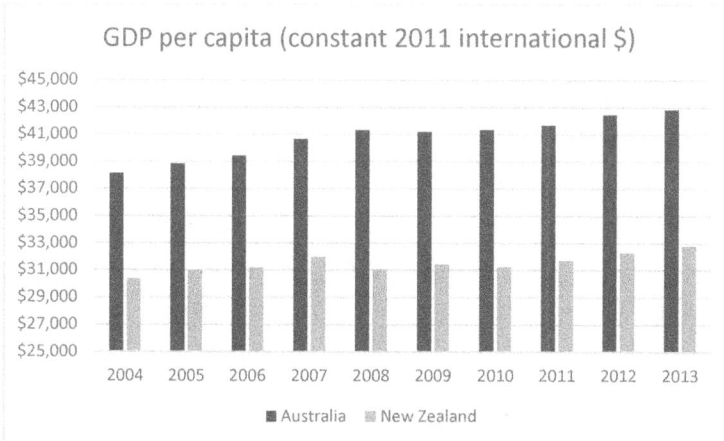

GDP per capita (constant 2011 international $)

Figure 5: Comparison of GDP per capita in constant 2011 international $
(Source: World Bank Development Indicators)

percent of the total population migrated to Australia. When this author moved from Sydney to Wellington in early 2012, it felt like swimming against the current. More than once the question was asked: Why would anyone in his right mind move from Australia to New Zealand?

At first glance, such questions were certainly justified and, indeed, are still justified. As Figure 5 shows, New Zealand's per capita GDP has been lagging behind Australia's for a long time. The New Zealand Productivity Commission summed up the comparative performance:

> Despite having broadly similar levels of institutional development and policy settings, GDP per capita in New Zealand has persistently diverged from Australia since the mid-1970s, when both countries had similar levels of average income. Comparatively low GDP per capita in New Zealand overwhelmingly reflects a poor performance in labour productivity, which has typically suffered a long slow decline vis-à-vis Australia and the OECD average for a number of decades.[44]

In rough terms New Zealand's per capita GDP has hovered at a level between a quarter and a third lower than Australia's for the past decade, with relatively little fluctuation. However, such comparisons should be treated with caution. Former Reserve Bank governor Allan Bollard repeatedly pointed out that when it comes to measuring economic output, New Zealand tends to take a very conservative approach while Australia tends to do the opposite. The Reserve Bank of New Zealand estimated in 2012 that after adjusting for the differences, the country's comparative per capita GDP was up to 10% higher than official data.[45] Nevertheless, whether New Zealand lags behind by 30 percent or by just 20 percent, there can be no doubt that there is a Trans-Tasman gap.

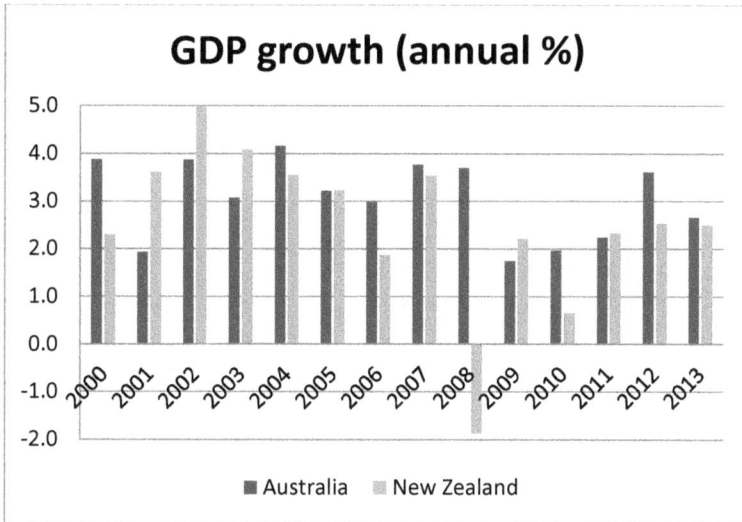

Figure 6: Comparison of GDP growth (annual %, source: World Bank Development Indicators)

When one looks at Australia's and New Zealand's growth performance since the turn of the century, however, there is not much between both countries on a per capita basis. Australia's average real GDP growth rate (the geometric mean) was 3 percent per year and New Zealand's 2.5 percent (Figure 6). However, since Australia recorded stronger population growth over this period than New Zealand, this translates into per capita GDP growth rates of 1.5 percent for Australia and 1.4 percent for New Zealand (Figure 7).

Judged over the longer period going back to the year 2000, Australia is narrowly ahead. As Figure 7 demonstrates, New Zealand has been growing somewhat faster than Australia since 2011. New Zealand experienced a dramatic decrease in per capita GDP during the Global Financial Crisis in 2008. It took New Zealand until 2012 to recover its per capita GDP to the 2007 level, whereas Australia's GDP per capita only suffered a minor loss in 2009.

GDP per capita growth (annual %)

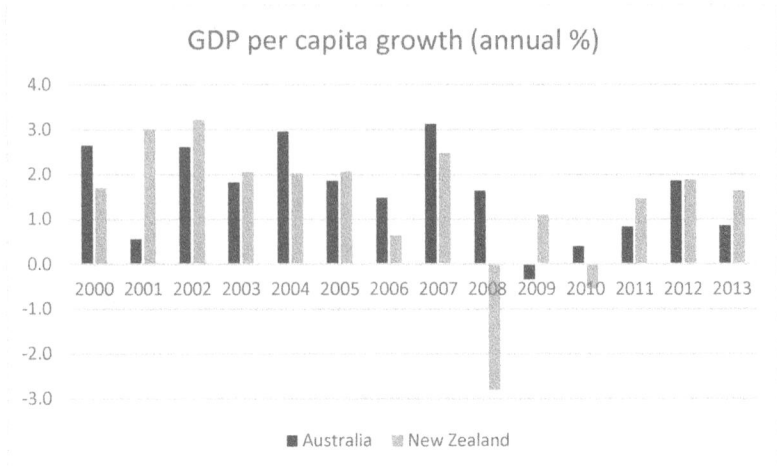

Figure 7: Comparison of GDP per capita growth (Source: World Bank Development Indicators)

While Australia has a medium-to-long-term edge over New Zealand when it comes to economic growth, New Zealand is outperforming Australia on measures of competitiveness and economic freedom. It is here that we can most clearly see the contrast between Australia's reform holiday and New Zealand's rediscovered reformist spirit.

Every year, the World Economic Forum (WEF) ranks 144 economies by their competitiveness. The WEF defines competitiveness as 'the set of institutions, policies, and factors that determine the level of productivity of a country.'[46] The index amalgamates a dozen measures of competitiveness: Institutions, Infrastructure, the Macroeconomic Environment, Health and Primary Education, Higher Education, Goods Market Efficiency, Labour Market Efficiency, Financial Market Development, Technological Readiness, Market Size, Business Sophistication and Innovation.

In the early 2000s, Australia ranked in the top 10 internationally, while New Zealand was ranked in the mid-teens (Figure 8). However, both countries suffered a deterioration in the following years. In Australia's case, it could be interpreted as the first effects of the reform holiday. For New Zealand it would appear to be due to more interventionist government under Labour Prime Minister Helen Clark. As a result, by 2011 Australia had fallen to 20th spot on the ladder and New Zealand was 25th.

The 2011/12 WEF Competitiveness Report marks a turning point for New Zealand. When the 2014/15 table was published in September 2014, it clawed back eight positions to 17th. Meanwhile Australia continued its decline and is now ranked 22nd. It is only the second time (after 2013) in the history of the WEF competitiveness index that New Zealand has outperformed Australia.

New Zealand is not only more competitive, it is also more economically liberal and has been for some time. The Fraser Institute in Canada has been measuring global economic freedom for many

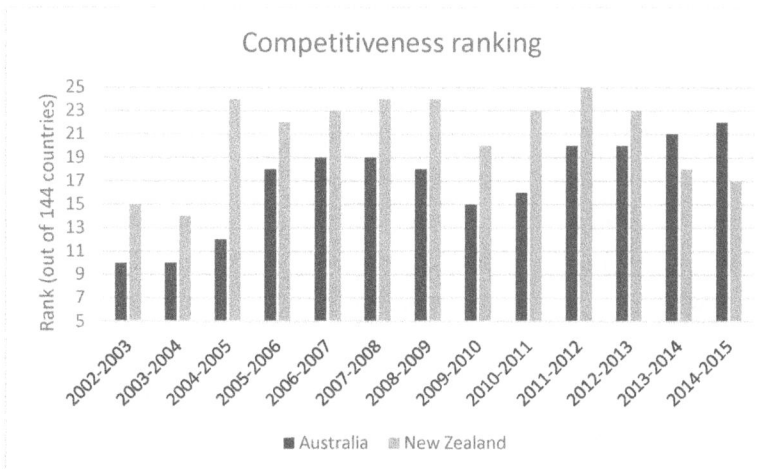

Figure 8: Comparison of rankings in the World Economic Forum's annual competitiveness index (out of 144 countries)

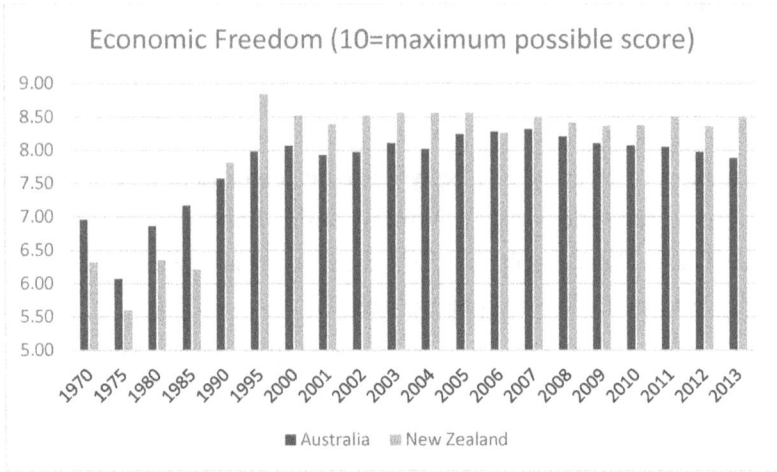

Figure 9: Comparison of economic freedom score in the Fraser Institute's Economic Freedom of the World index

years. Figure 9 shows that before the economic reforms under Hawke/Keating in Australia and Roger Douglas in New Zealand, both countries could hardly be described as liberal economies. The situation in New Zealand, especially under Prime Minister Robert Muldoon, was certainly worse; Labour prime minister David Lange went so far as to describe the economy as 'being run very similarly to a Polish shipyard'.

The economic reforms undertaken by both countries in the 1980s and 1990s were more radical in New Zealand than in Australia. New Zealand abolished almost all agricultural subsidies virtually overnight, for example, while Australia, notwithstanding its other economic reforms, continued to run generous subsidies for industries such as car manufacturing.

The economic freedom measure demonstrates that Australia has been on the decline for some years. It achieved its best score – 8.32 out of 10 – in 2007, but by 2013 it only measured 7.33. New Zealand, on the other hand, scored a low of 8.36 in 2009 but has since recovered to a score of 8.49 in 2013. New Zealand is now the third freest economy in the world and only surpassed by the city states of Hong Kong and Singapore. Australia, on the other hand, now has a freedom score that more resembles the freer European economies.

There is a paradox, then, since New Zealand's better score for economic freedom over Australia does not translate (yet) into better economic performance compared to other developed economies. This inconsistency has become known as New Zealand's *productivity paradox* and it means that New Zealand's GDP per capita is currently 12 percent lower than the OECD average. Given the country's policy settings, however, in areas such as taxation, labour markets and product markets, New Zealand's GDP per capita would be expected to be about 20% higher than the OECD average (Figure 6, 2009 data).

There is considerable academic literature about the reasons for New Zealand's underperformance. The New Zealand Productivity

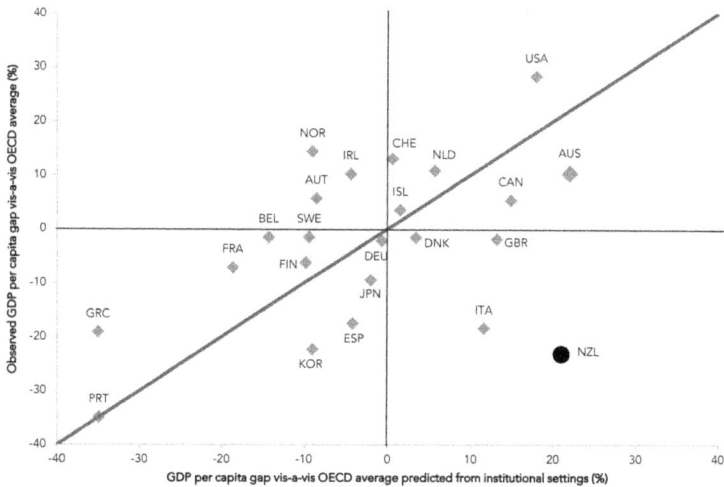

Figure 10: Observed gap in GDP/capita versus the gap predicted from structural policies, 2009

Commission identifies a gap in knowledge-based capital and the disadvantage in economic geography among the main factors. This is not the place to enter into the debate about the productivity paradox as such but merely to suggest another factor explaining the divergence between Australia's and New Zealand's economic performance in recent years: the two countries' respective terms-of-trade.

In economics, terms-of-trade are defined as the relation between export and import prices. Australia benefitted enormously from the industrialisation of Asian economies over the past two decades, which was reflected in rising prices for the commodities Australia exported while prices for import goods fell. Reserve Bank of Australia governor provided a very neat illustration in a speech in 2010:

> Five years ago, a ship load of iron ore was worth about the same as about 2,200 flat screen television sets. Today it is worth about 22,000 flat-screen TV sets – partly due to TV prices falling but more due to the price of iron ore rising by a factor of six.[48]

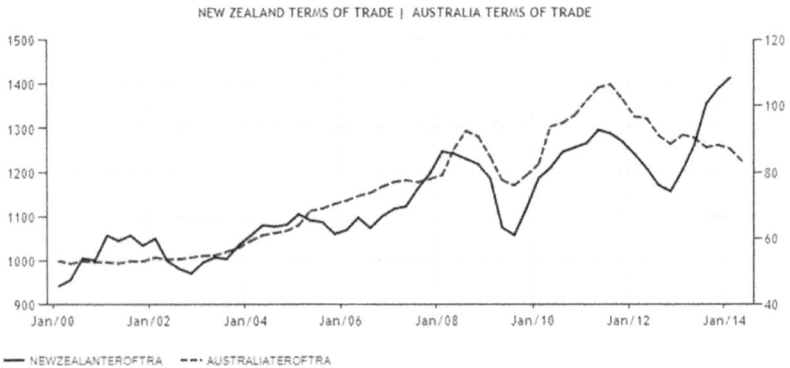

Figure 11: Comparison of Terms of Trade (Source: tradingeconomics.com)

Australia delivered the hard commodities that are needed in the initial stages of industrialisation. For New Zealand, however, primarily an exporter of agricultural products, the terms-of-trade boom occurred later as Asian economies entered a more consumption-driven phase. As Figure 11 shows, Australia's terms-of-trade have declined since 2012 while New Zealand's are close to all-time highs.

When comparing the performance of the two economies since Key took office, one should keep these developments in mind. New Zealand is still lagging behind Australia when it comes to GDP per capita, New Zealand now looks the more competitive and freer of the two economies, notwithstanding the fact that Australian government spending as a ratio of GDP is still smaller than in New Zealand. It reflects both Australia's competitive decline and New Zealand's more recent reforms. At the same time, New Zealand is benefitting from a terms-of-trade boom which Australia used to enjoy but does not do so anymore.

In short: We may be witnessing a role reversal in Australia's and New Zealand's economic fortunes, for which there is not a single reason but a multitude of factors at work, some of them external. As described earlier, the Key government certainly deserves some credit for New Zealand's better performance.

Reform and leadership

At a time when many Australian and international commentators are giving up on the possibility of implementing reforms in mature democracies, New Zealand has demonstrated they are still possible. The New Zealand experience, however, also shows how difficult it is to change the political course in the face of public and institutional inertia.

The price the New Zealand government pays for working through its reform agenda is its incrementalism; the price the New Zealand public pays for this incrementalism are the opportunity costs of waste and inefficiency that could have been avoided by faster reforms.

To the frustration of political pundits, economic advisors, at least one prominent think tank, and some former politicians, the Key government's reforms do not come as a 'big bang' with strident rhetoric but more like a finely crafted, slow process. It is reminiscent of Max Weber's 1919 essay 'Politics as a vocation':

> Politics is a strong and slow boring of hard boards. It takes both passion and perspective. Certainly all historical experience confirms the truth – that man would not have attained the possible unless time and again he had reached out for the impossible. But to do that a man must be a leader, and not only a leader but a hero as well, in a very sober

sense of the word. And even those who are neither leaders
nor heroes must arm themselves with that steadfastness of
heart which can brave even the crumbling of all hopes. This
is necessary right now, or else men will not be able to attain
even that which is possible today.[49]

It is certainly true that politics is still 'a strong and slow boring
of hard boards'. The difference between the ideal politician that
Weber described almost a century ago and the current New Zealand
government is that Key never appears to reach for the impossible
but keeps focussed firmly on the achievable. That, perhaps, is
why Key has managed to implement reforms that have eluded
Australian governments for years.

New Zealand's future prosperity depends, as always, on
the degree to which public opinion will support productivity-
enhancing reforms and on the quality of political leadership in
building constituencies for reform and implementing acceptable
reforms. Key has made his judgments about those issues, and his
success must command the respect of those who understand how
hard the reform path is.

It will be left to historians to decide if Key really was the heroic
leader that New Zealand needed, or merely the best Prime Minister
that circumstances would allow.

So what, if anything, could Australia learn from New Zealand's
reform experience under the Key government? Similar as they
are in many other respects, there are some significant institutional
differences that might suggest that New Zealand as a country is
more easily reformed than Australia.

New Zealand's population is one-fifth of Australia's. Smaller
countries could be easier to turn around than large ones, not

least because large countries have a more complex structure of political institutions and better organised and more vocal interest groups.

However, this argument might also run the other way: that the greater degree of anonymity in larger countries makes it possible to ignore small interest groups and vocal opponents. At least in this author's impression, small size rather breeds consensus – for a very simple reason: In countries like New Zealand you have to be careful when making enemies because you always meet twice (if not more often).

Size in itself, therefore, is not necessarily a good predictor of 'reformability' but there are other institutional differences that could weigh in favour of New Zealand's ability to change. New Zealand might benefit from the fact that it is neither a federal system, nor does it practice bicameralism.

As much as federalism and bicameralism are helpful in providing checks and balances on power, when it comes to implementing reforms they complicate the picture. Even the most reform-minded administrations struggle against a hostile Senate or politically opposed state governments. In this regard, an elected New Zealand government certainly has it easier: once in power, it is in a much stronger position than its Australian counterpart.

That advantage, however, must be balanced against the difficulties posed by New Zealand's Mixed Member Proportional electoral system. Forming government is much harder under MMP than in countries using a Westminster-style first-past-the-post or Australia's single transferable vote system. In New Zealand, as in other MMP countries, coalition governments are the rule, not the exception. In Germany, for example, only one government since

1949 was elected with an absolute majority. In all other elections, coalitions were needed to govern. The same is true for New Zealand, and even in John Key's spectacular election success in 2014, his party was still one parliamentary seat short to govern in its own right.

Since 2008, the National-led government of John Key therefore depended on confidence-and-supply support from the ACT, United Future and Māori parties. Getting these four somewhat diverse parties to agree can sometimes outweigh the complexities imposed by federalism and bicameralism on Australian federal governments. Or put differently, New Zealand may have once been a highly reformable country but since the introduction of MMP it has become much harder to implement any majority party's agenda. (Ironically, Key could have changed this but failed to campaign effectively for a return to the first-past-the-post system which was on the cards in a referendum held in parallel with the 2011 election.) This means that he has effectively made it harder for himself to win elections and govern more independently. The convoluted electoral system under which New Zealand operates is a veritable nightmare in its own right.

While some Australian commentators have singled out the media as one of the factors preventing reform, the New Zealand media do not quite appear to be the flag-bearers of reform either. The number of media commentators and columnists regularly making the case for change, greater productivity and more economically liberal policies can be counted on one hand. Perhaps New Zealand radio stations and newspapers may be less strident than their Australian counterparts (though this is hard to judge objectively), but it would be fair to say that the New Zealand media is not the driving force behind economic reforms.

In summary, there are no good reasons why Australia should not or could not be compared to New Zealand. Differences in political landscapes do not sufficiently explain the differing patterns of reform. Both governments face headwinds. It would appear to be a universal truth, as Gough Whitlam once said, that 'the way of the reformer is hard.'[50]

So what are the lessons the Australian government may want to consider from Key's example? Having analysed the Key government's behaviour over its first two terms in power, there are four P's which emerge: Patience, Preparation, Pragmatism and Principle. These are the guidelines under which the current New Zealand government operates. They are its 'Key values' – but not all of them seem to be Abbott's values (just yet):

Patience – The Key government did not try to do everything at once. It waited until the time was right to introduce reforms, and when it did so it introduced these reforms one by one, bit by bit. Only over time did these puzzle pieces come together as a more coherent picture of where Key wanted to take his country. In Australia, on the other hand, an impatient Abbott government tried too many things at once, especially in its first Budget. This may have been understandable because at least from Abbott's perspective, Australia had been going in the wrong direction and once in office, he wanted to turn it around. However, in doing so, his government did not succeed in building a narrative for its actions, nor did it manage to convince the public of the necessity of its policy measures. The introduction of GP co-payments is a good example. What may have made sense as part of a package of health reforms became regarded as a symbol of rushed policy-making that landed on an unprepared nation apparently out of the blue. It was a gift to Bill Shorten's Opposition and hostile commentators who, in the absence of a clear narrative from the government, swiftly constructed their own. To successfully sell such measures to the public takes considerably more time than the Abbott government allowed and a longer conversation. We may be wishing to change the world over night but it usually requires more patience than that.

Preparation – A government that wants its reforms to have lasting success needs to establish consensus around them. Only if a majority of the public understands and accepts the need for change, will they go with it. To achieve this consensus, it takes careful preparation. John Key's government has demonstrated how this works, using external working groups, institutions like the Productivity Commission and strong and credible ministers like Paula Bennett and Bill English to lay the foundations for future reform. The Abbott government, in its first year, often did not appear to be preparing any next steps and rather went straight to the implementation stage. In hindsight, this was a mistake – as Abbott now appears to recognise. In his October 2014 speech in Tenterfield he canvassed major reforms to the federal system but added:

> Without a measure of consensus, any change requiring legislation is unlikely to secure parliamentary passage and the whole exercise could turn out to be futile. Without an element of consensus, any change that's actually achieved could be reversed at the earliest opportunity and therefore hardly worth doing.[51]

This is precisely right – and it is precisely what John Key has been practicing for six years.

Pragmatism – Key would never forgo an opportunity to make things better just because he could not make them perfect. He is willing to go for second-best solution if that is the only thing achievable for the time being. Even second-best solutions can still be perfected over time (which, again, requires preparation and patience). It is an understanding of politics as the art of the possible which no-one better personifies than John Key. The Abbott government seems to be moving in this direction as well judging from its preparedness to cut deals in the Senate to ensure the passage of contentious legislation.

Principles – As much as principles are often ineffective with pragmatism, pragmatism on its own is blind without principles. Key's government could afford to be pragmatic because it had clarity over the direction in which it wanted to go in the long run (even though they do not often engage in the rhetoric of reform). There is a world of difference, therefore, between pragmatism and 'muddling through'. Reformist pragmatism needs to be informed by firmly-held economic beliefs. A political leader with both pragmatism and principles has a good chance of achieving substantial change over time.

Patience, Preparation, Pragmatism and Principles: These are the tools that should be at the command of any reforming political leader.

There is a fifth P, though, which is vital for any reform. It is a quality that both John Key and Tony Abbott possess, and it is Passion. It is the passion to change their countries for the better. John Key is as often talking about his passion for New Zealand as Tony Abbott is talking about his passion for Australia.

If Abbott is to become a reforming prime minister, he must first solve what Paul Kelly calls 'the Australian crisis': the polarisation of politics, the evaporation of consensus and the deterioration of process. Kelly notes 'the apparent abandonment of the proven techniques of inquiry, debate, consultation and compromise.'[52] It is a task Abbott explicitly embraced when he launched Kelly's *Triumph and Demise* in August 2014: 'Our challenge – the challenge of the current Government – is to show that the age of reform has not ended, it was merely interrupted.'[53]

Ultimately, Australia's future prosperity depends on Abbott's success in achieving just that. If he requires any ideas for this daunting task, a look across the Tasman may well be inspirational. The adoption of the New Zealand method of quiet, incremental radicalism may be Australia's best hope of rediscovering the art of reform.

Endnotes

1 Australia votes yes for competent government, *The Australian*, 9 September 2013, http://www.theaustralian.com.au/opinion/editorials/australia-votes-yes-for-competent-government/story-e6frg71x-1226714801300

2 Paul Kelly, *The End of Certainty: Power, Politics and Business in Australia*, Sydney: Allen & Unwin, 1994.

3 John Howard, *Lazarus Rising: A Personal and Political Autobiography*, Sydney: Harper Collins, 2010, pp. 302-316.

4 Tony Makin, *Australia's Competitiveness: Reversing the Slide*, Canberra: Minerals Council of Australia, 2014, pp. 51-61.

5 Lindsay Tanner, *Sideshow: Dumbing down democracy*, Melbourne: Scribe, 2011.

6 Paul Kelly, *Triumph and Demise: The broken promise of a Labor generation*, Melbourne: Melbourne University Press, 2014.

7 Jean-Claude Juncker's most outrageous political quotations, *The Daily Telegraph* (London), 15 July 2014, http://www.telegraph.co.uk/news/worldnews/europe/eu/10967168/Jean-Claude-Junckers-most-outrageous-political-quotations.html

8 There's much Tony Abbott could learn from John Key's triumph in NZ, *The Australian*, 22 September 2014, http://www.theaustralian.com.au/opinion/columnists/theres-much-tony-abbott-could-learn-from-john-keys-triumph-in-nz/story-fn7078da-1227065791798

9 Team Key teaches lessons on democracy to Team Australia, *Sydney Morning Herald*, 23 September 2014, http://www.smh.com.au/comment/team-key-teaches-lessons-on-democracy-to-team-australia-20140922-10kgv3.html

10 The meaning of election 2014, *The National Business Review*, 26 September 2014.

11 *Victorious New Zealand PM pledges more of the same, eyes 4th term*, Yahoo News, 21 September 2014, http://news.yahoo.com/polls-open-zealand-election-212405219.html

[12] Luke Malpass, Land of the long white cloud faces bad weather, *The Age*, 24 November 2011.

[13] The Welfare Working Group's Terms of Reference, Issues Paper and Options Paper are available at http://ips.ac.nz/WelfareWorkingGroup/Index.html

[14] *Govt readies welfare reforms*, Stuff.co.nz, 30 May 2011, http://www.stuff.co.nz/national/politics/5075646/Govt-readies-welfare-reforms

[15] Simon Collins, Cabinet's new poster girl, *The New Zealand Herald*, 22 November 2008, http://www.nzherald.co.nz/nz-election-2008/news/article.cfm?c_id=1501799&objectid=10544395&pnum=0

[16] See Work and Income, *New benefit categories – 15 July 2013*, http://www.workandincome.govt.nz/individuals/benefit-changes/new-benefit-categories.html

[17] New Zealand government press release, *Welfare reform legislation to be introduced*, 27 February 2012, http://www.beehive.govt.nz/release/welfare-reform-legislation-be-introduced

[18] New Zealand government press release, *Investment approach refocuses entire welfare system*, 12 September 2012, http://www.beehive.govt.nz/release/investment-approach-refocuses-entire-welfare-system

[19] New Zealand government press release, *Welfare numbers lowest since 2008*, 18 July 2014, http://www.beehive.govt.nz/release/welfare-numbers-lowest-2008

[20] Ministry of Social Development, All main benefits – September 2014 quarter, http://www.msd.govt.nz/about-msd-and-our-work/publications-resources/statistics/benefit/post-sep-2013/all-main-benefits/september-2014-quarter.html

[21] Ministry for Social Development, Annual Report 2013/14, Wellington, October 2014, p. 14, http://www.msd.govt.nz/documents/about-msd-and-our-work/publications-resources/corporate/annual-report/2014/annual-report-2013-2014.pdf

[22] State Services Commission, *Better Public Services: Reducing long-term welfare dependence*, 8 July 2014, https://www.ssc.govt.nz/bps-reducing-dependence

[23] Auckland Action against Poverty media release, *Beneficiaries receive biggest boot in the guts since '91*, 9 April 2013, http://aaap.org.nz/2013/04/10/beneficiaries-receive-biggest-boot-in-the-guts-since-91-cuts/

[24] Welfare reforms a 'death blow to social contract' – *Labour, One News*, 10 April 2013, http://tvnz.co.nz/politics-news/welfare-reforms-death-blow-social-contract-labour-5400610

[25] Oliver Hartwich, Germany's global ranking is a teachable moment, *Australian Financial Review*, 13 September 2013, http://www.afr.com/p/lifestyle/review/germany_global_ranking_is_teachable_UMUYaupoJr0hORl26a1AfP

[26] New Zealand Treasury, *Economic and Fiscal Forecasts December 2008*, Wellington, 18 December 2008, http://www.treasury.govt.nz/budget/forecasts/eff2008

[27] NZ's foreign debt outlook downgraded by S & P, *New Zealand Herald*, 13 January 2009, http://www.nzherald.co.nz/fiscal-policy/news/article.cfm?c_id=203&objectid=10551702

[28] OECD has tough remedies for NZ, *New Zealand Herald*, 18 April 2009, http://www.nzherald.co.nz/fiscal-policy/news/article.cfm?c_id=203&objectid=10567229

[29] International Monetary Fund, *New Zealand: 2009 Article IV Consultation – Staff Report; Public Information Notice on the Executive Board Discussion*, Washington, 2009, p. 10.

[30] Christchurch rebuild to cost $10b more, *3News*, 28 April 2013, http://www.3news.co.nz/politics/christchurch-rebuild-to-cost-10b-more-2013042813

[31] Levy to pay for $5.6b flood bill, *Sydney Morning Herald*, 27 January 2011, http://www.smh.com.au/business/levy-to-pay-for-56b-flood-bill-20110127-1a64x.html

[32] Robert Higgs, *Crisis and Leviathan: Critical Episodes in the Growth of American Government*, Oxford/New York: Oxford University Press, 1987.

[33] New Zealand Treasury, *Pre-election Economic and Fiscal Update 2014*, August 2014, http://www.treasury.govt.nz/budget/forecasts/prefu2014

[34] $42bn package to head off recession, *The Australian*, 3 February 2009, http://www.theaustralian.com.au/archive/business/bn-package-to-head-off-recession/story-e6frgagx-1111118741863

[35] Bill English, *Budget sets out New Zealand's road to recovery*, 28 May 2009, http://www.beehive.govt.nz/release/budget-sets-out-new-zealand%E2%80%99s-road-recovery-main-summary

[36] *National-ACT Confidence-and-Supply Agreement 2008*, Wellington, 16 November 2008, http://www.act.org.nz/files/agreement.pdf

[37] *9th Annual Demographia International Housing Affordability Survey*, Christchurch: Performance Urban Planning, 2013.

[38] International Monetary Fund, *IMF Executive Board Concludes 2014 Article IV Consultation with New Zealand* (press release), 9 June 2014, http://www.imf.org/external/np/sec/pr/2014/pr14271.htm

[39] Rodney Hide, Flag debate is next poll distraction, *National Business Review*, 11 October 2014, http://www.nbr.co.nz/article/flag-debate-next-poll-distraction

[40] Bryce Edwards, The next three years of National boredom, *New Zealand Herald*, 22 October 2014, http://www.nzherald.co.nz/politics/news/article.cfm?c_id=280&objectid=11346602

[41] In his autobiography, Don Brash shares his frustration about an economically illiterate public in which prejudice over the achievements of Rogernomics still prevails: Don Brash, *Incredible Luck*, Auckland: Troika, 2014, pp. 259-292.

[42] Parata defends class size backdown, *3 News*, 8 June 2012, http://www.3news.co.nz/politics/parata-defends-class-size-backdown-2012060809

[43] See for example Andrew Patterson, David Kirk, Don Turkington and Luke Malpass, *Flight of the Kiwi: Addressing the Brain Drain*, Sydney: The Centre for Independent Studies, 2012.

[44] Paul Conway, Lisa Meehan and Guanyu Zheng, *New Zealand Productivity Commission Staff Working Paper 2013/1: How integrated are the Australian and New Zealand economies?*, Wellington: New Zealand Productivity Commission, 2013, p. 2.

[45] *Could we be better off than we think?*, Reserve Bank of New Zealand media release, 17 February *2012*, http://www.rbnz.govt.nz/news/2012/4683280.html. See also Alan Bollard and Rochelle Barrow, *Could we be better off than we think? A speech delivered to Trans-Tasman Business Circle in Auckland*, 17 February 2012, http://www.rbnz.govt.nz/research_and_publications/speeches/2012/4683869.pdf

[46] World Economic Forum, http://www.weforum.org/issues/global-competitiveness

[47] Alain de Serres, Naomitsu Yashiro and Hervé Boulhol, *An International Perspective on the New Zealand Productivity Paradox*, New Zealand Productivity Commission Working Paper 2014/01, Wellington, 2014, p. 2.

[48] Glenn Stevens, *The Challenge of Prosperity: Address to the Committee for Economic Development of Australia (CEDA)* Annual Dinner Melbourne – 29 November 2010, http://www.rba.gov.au/speeches/2010/sp-gov-291110.html

[49] Max Weber, *Politik als Beruf*, 1919 (republished Max Weber, *Gesammelte Politische Schriften*, 5th edition, Tübingen: Mohr 1988, pp. 505-560).

[50] Gough Whitlam, *Ben Chifley Memorial Lecture*, 19 July 1957.

[51] Tony Abbott, *Speech at the Sir Henry Parkes Commemorative Dinner*, 25 October 2014.

[52] Paul Kelly, *Triumph and Demise: The Broken Promise of a Labor Generation*, Melbourne University Press, Melbourne, 2014, p. 508.

[53] Tony Abbott, *Address to launch 'Triumph and Demise' book*, 26 August 2014.

Appendix 1

Hope is not a strategy

Bill English

Where will we look for new directions and ideas? To be frank – they will not come from Australia and New Zealand. In our countries, the prevailing public management literature and approach is conditioned by a decade of generous year-on-year increases in funding.

However, it is impossible to ignore the fact that globally public sector management is entering its next revolution. That revolution will be driven by the large economic and geopolitical changes that are taking place as many Western governments grapple with the aftershocks of the global recession.

The public sectors in the countries we usually compare ourselves with – the United States, the UK and much of Europe – will spend the next two decades dealing with the consequences of large government deficits and high and fast growing public debt. As a result of the global financial crisis, changes that may have taken 20 years to occur will happen in five years. This is a significant shift.

The last decade was characterised by optimism that smart people using the massive resources of government could transform society. That experiment has run out of money and has little that is genuinely transformational to show for it. The new experiments will have less aspirational goals – sorting out which public services and income support measures really matter and working out how to do it for a lot less money.

I believe we will see radical changes in the scope and cost of public services in the UK, United States and most of Europe. They have no choice. However, at the same time as the global financial crisis has inflicted large debts on some governments, many fast emerging economies in the developing world are travelling in the opposite direction. These countries, which are generating large surpluses as their economies rapidly expand, are likely to develop stronger consumer and service economies, along with a demand for more public services.

Most of these countries are starting with low levels of income support and minimal government provision of public services. India and Africa are now developing sufficiently consistent economic growth to stimulate demand for public services.

They too will be looking for solutions and creating experiments. Australia and New Zealand will not be at the cutting edge of either of these revolutions. Our role may be to sell our frameworks for accountability and transparency to the emerging economies developing their public services, while borrowing some of the cost-crunching innovations that are developed in the UK, United States and Europe.

In New Zealand, we are laying the foundations for a public service that chooses innovation and change. I want to first describe how we are thinking about the next five years and discuss some of the factors we believe will drive further change – as well as the core public sector management system change that will be required.

Faced with fast growing deficits, we have chosen what I call the 'responsibility model'. As an incoming government, we had a choice to make savings across the board and restructure the public service to get efficiencies. However, we have left existing structures largely in place, and set out clear fiscal constraints for the next four years. We have pushed responsibility for managing resources clearly on to public sector chief executives, rather than the Treasury or the Minister of Finance.

So rather than embarking on wholesale change, we are stress testing the existing devolved model of public sector management. There are two reasons for this. The 2008 election was fought in the world before the global financial crisis.

Then, in Opposition, we made undertakings to leave existing income support measures in place, and to focus on moving public sector resources from the back office to the frontline. This positioning effectively ruled out rationing public services or pushing more cost back on to the public. So that is not a debate we are entering into.

Instead, we are focused on getting value for money from the current level of resources. In this context, we also specifically ruled out large-scale structural change and we have kept to those undertakings, despite the change in circumstances.

The second reason is that New Zealand's previous experience of fiscal restraint shows that longer-term effective change is driven by people who know the business, clearly understand the parameters they are working to and have the tools they need to implement change.

So chief executives – not the Cabinet or the Treasury – are responsible for delivering better services and policy advice with less money and fewer people.

This model requires ministers and chief executives to clarify the results they want.

We are using the basic tools of ministerial and chief executive accountability, not inventing new ones. We spend time on the Prime Minister's expectations of ministers, and getting ministers to focus clearly on their expectations of their chief executives. These expectations are driven off pragmatic political commitments and clearly understood fiscal constraints. This process needs constant reinforcement to maintain focus over time. And it takes time to build momentum.

The culture of caution and risk management in the public sector has been deeply embedded in the last 10 years. So the Government has to keep demonstrating political support for change, and mandating tools chief executives can use without fear of political consequences.

In practice, the challenges are predictable. The first is that everyone in the public sector hopes the rules will change – in particular that politicians won't stick to self-imposed spending constraints. Some are still trying to wait it out.

However, it's not an option for the public sector to wait out these challenges. Hope is not a strategy. And it won't work because the New Zealand public wants to see evidence that the public sector is living within its means, as New Zealanders are themselves. So the political case for staying the course, for constraint and better value for money, remains strong in New Zealand.

Second, in a devolved system, it takes time and effort to get the balance between collective and individual interests among ministers. This is more of a challenge in a centre right Government, where ministers tend to come from self-employed or business backgrounds.

Ministers have impressive degrees of freedom to do, or not do things. So it is vital to achieve a strong common understanding of our collective purpose, and to turn this understanding into clearly aligned processes of accountability. And we need to achieve this within the political timetable of a three-year election cycle.

A third challenge is whether our public management system permits the kind of solutions that are now required. Solutions such as shared services, joint procurement, or joint decision making across a sector have not fitted naturally into our framework. In the last 20 years, there have been many attempts at joined up or collaborative government. Most, but not all, attempts have failed because the processes of joining up can be very inefficient and large committees collaborating do not make for strong accountability.

So it's a challenge for the public service to develop strong internal governance to run joint processes – in our case without strong central processes to dictate to them. In our approach, Cabinet has supported a handful of collective processes for the public sector, such as joint procurement and – beginning soon – administrative and support services benchmarking, as well as shared services in the health sector. We have also set up an internal infrastructure unit to create better capital management and project assessment. In each of these examples, chief executives have the choice of picking up the tool and using it, or not.

Progress has been slow to start with. But momentum is now picking up as chief executives understand they will need to take action as they see the growing gap over the next four years (our projection period) between rising costs and flat revenue. At the same time, voluntary participation in collective initiatives keeps a healthy tension on the proponents to show value for the time and effort.

We are beginning to see more collective activity among these independent chief executives, which shows the public service is developing a sense that it wants to influence its own destiny. That is because they understand the world has changed and that the only other viable alternative is politicians and the Treasury, armed with public support, going in and finding the savings themselves.

However, the governance of joint back office savings exercises is just a first step. The next step is to fulfil the theory of our public management system by setting outcomes and structuring accountability and governance around those outcomes.

Currently, governance and accountability are driven by the parliamentary appropriations process. That process accounts for the money, but not the results. Resolving the tension between parliamentary accountability and effective management for outcomes is one of the biggest challenges for the New Zealand public service. We need far-reaching solutions to make the far-reaching change dictated by fiscal constraint and public expectations.

One example is the criminal justice system. At a time when funding is tight, we have to find ways to foot the bill for tougher sentences for serious criminals, which the public demands. One response is to reduce offending and prosecution and imprisonment rates for less serious offenders.

Over recent years, justice sector agencies have begun to work together to understand better who gets arrested and why, how they move through the police and courts system to prison or otherwise and at what cost. This has generated at least some initial operational solutions for a more effective and more just system.

But driving these changes further will require something even more difficult than good political management. It will require joint governance and accountability in what is currently a strongly siloed system.

The politicians' task is to turn the objective of community safety into some high level outcomes, like reduced prison numbers, or reduced youth offending rates. The public service needs to think about the governance and accountability structure that can drive decisions to achieve these outcomes.

We have any amount of policy analysis and any amount of public support for success. But there is very little accumulated wisdom on what governance and accountability will deliver the desired policy result.

In this sector, as with many others, we simply won't meet the fiscal constraints and public expectations with the current institutional arrangements.

You will hear debate about these issues across a number of sectors in the next few years – long-term welfare, delivery of social services, housing, defence and others.

The last decade has seen an excess of cash and confidence in the public sector. The results of large dollops of both are not impressive – government is bigger, but core social problems remain intractable, and voters are sceptical that their cash has been well used.

The benign economic conditions of the last decade will not occur again for decades, so we face permanent fiscal constraint.

Ask this question: Has the way we think about public services and public policy changed as rapidly as the world around us? The answer is no, not yet, but larger forces of economics, technology and public demand mean our thinking will have to change.

In New Zealand, we have chosen a path of considered and consistent change over time and engaging the leadership of the public service in the mission of significantly changing the way we do business.

I am confident that if we use the tools available, and draw on a wider range of resource outside the public service, we will succeed in the immediate task of meeting reasonable public expectations with fewer resources.

We also have a larger obligation to the next generation. Fewer of them will be supporting more of us as we leave the workforce.

The cost of inertia and inaction will be a double burden of large public debt and an ageing population. We owe it to them to innovate, to take risks, to push the boundaries and to pay our own way. The clock is ticking.

Speech to the Australia New Zealand School of Government Annual Conference, 12 August 2010.

Appendix 2

What governments can (and cannot) do
to grow national prosperity.

Joe Hockey

As someone with a bit of Kiwi blood myself thanks to my Bay of Islands born grandmother, I have a special affinity for New Zealanders.

The Australia-New Zealand story is as much about shared values as it is about friendly sibling rivalry, particularly on the rugby pitch. We have a mutual ambition for our nations.

New Zealand has stolen the advantage from Australia over the last few years by combining domestic structural reforms with newly negotiated trade opportunities in Asia. As a result, they have falling unemployment, rising living standards and a Budget that is coming into surplus.

New Zealand has not achieved this through luck or complacency; there is no 'she'll be right' attitude, there. They are not blessed with an abundance of energy and resources like Australia. New Zealand's success has come through the delivery of necessary economic reforms. Even with the advantage of a single Parliamentary Chamber, the delivery of reform has been a great credit for Prime Minister, John Key, Deputy Prime Minister Bill English and their New Zealand National Party colleagues.

New Zealand is showing the world how economic reform should be done.

Despite being a small open economy, the nation did undertake structural reform at the most opportune time – even though it was done against an incredibly difficult backdrop. With the full impact of the Global Financial Crisis and the devastating Christchurch earthquake, and the rebuild cost almost 20 per cent of GDP, the National Government is on track to deliver a return to fiscal surplus over the coming year.

Since 2010, New Zealand's Budget balance has improved by 7.5 per cent of GDP. Australia's fiscal consolidation since then has been around one third of that.

New Zealand has done this through careful use of public resources, sound economic policies, and a commitment to improving the quality of public services.

Like Australia, it set out a credible path back to surplus and to paying down debt – but most importantly it was able to stick to that path. That means the Government can spend more money on things New Zealanders actually need like roads and ports rather than using their taxes to pay interest on debt.

In New Zealand, the sustained public sector efficiency improvements, the reprioritisation of the government balance sheet, and changes to entitlements on schemes such as student loans, retirement savings, and welfare are all impressive achievements. As the New Zealand Deputy Prime Minister has said to me multiple times 'you have to fix the roof when the sun is shining'. It is logical to make the tough changes when times are relatively good because it is much more difficult to make meaningful changes in times of crisis.

New Zealand also recognises that reform is an ongoing process. Reform must not end with achieving a surplus – a surplus is only part of the ever continuing reform story.

In New Zealand, the Government's core expenses have come down from over 35 per cent of GDP in 2011 to a forecast 30 per cent in the coming year. This compares with our expenses, which have increased over the same period by around one per cent of GDP. Last month [July 2014] Fitch Ratings revised up their outlook for the New Zealand sovereign credit rating from stable to positive.

New Zealand's unemployment rate is forecast to fall by almost a percentage point over the next couple of years. Unemployment currently sits at the same level as Australia at six per cent. But while our rate is forecast to rise to six and a quarter per cent for the June Quarter of 2015, New Zealand's is forecast to drop to around 5.4 per cent by then.

So, the New Zealand population is benefiting from a stronger economy, more jobs, and a Government that lives within its means. It is also making itself a more attractive investment destination with a top personal tax rate of just 33 per cent, no payroll tax and I understand no land tax either.

Partly as a result of this there has been a significant turnaround in trans-Tasman migration flows over the past year. For the first time in years, more New Zealanders are returning from Australia than are departing to Australia. Kiwis are going home – and staying home – because times are good.

I commend you, Bill, for what you and your colleagues have achieved. You are changing the size and scope of government to build prosperity in New Zealand.

It is these sorts of results, coming from sound economic and fiscal stewardship, which the Abbott Government is working to achieve for the Australian people.

Australia has been missing from the reform party for much of the past few years – but we can catch up. Governments must adapt to new 'disruptive' technologies, new industries and a changed mindset of our citizens. The Government's role is changing from an initiator of change, to a facilitator of change.

Australian Governments have not taken the opportunities to facilitate that change in recent years. We now have the opportunity to build the environment for long-term prosperity and we must take it.

Speech to the Australia New Zealand School of Government Annual Conference, 6 August 2014.